I0485432

Copyright © 2015 Jessie Numbers

All Rights Reserved Worldwide

MEGA MANDALA MONSTERS

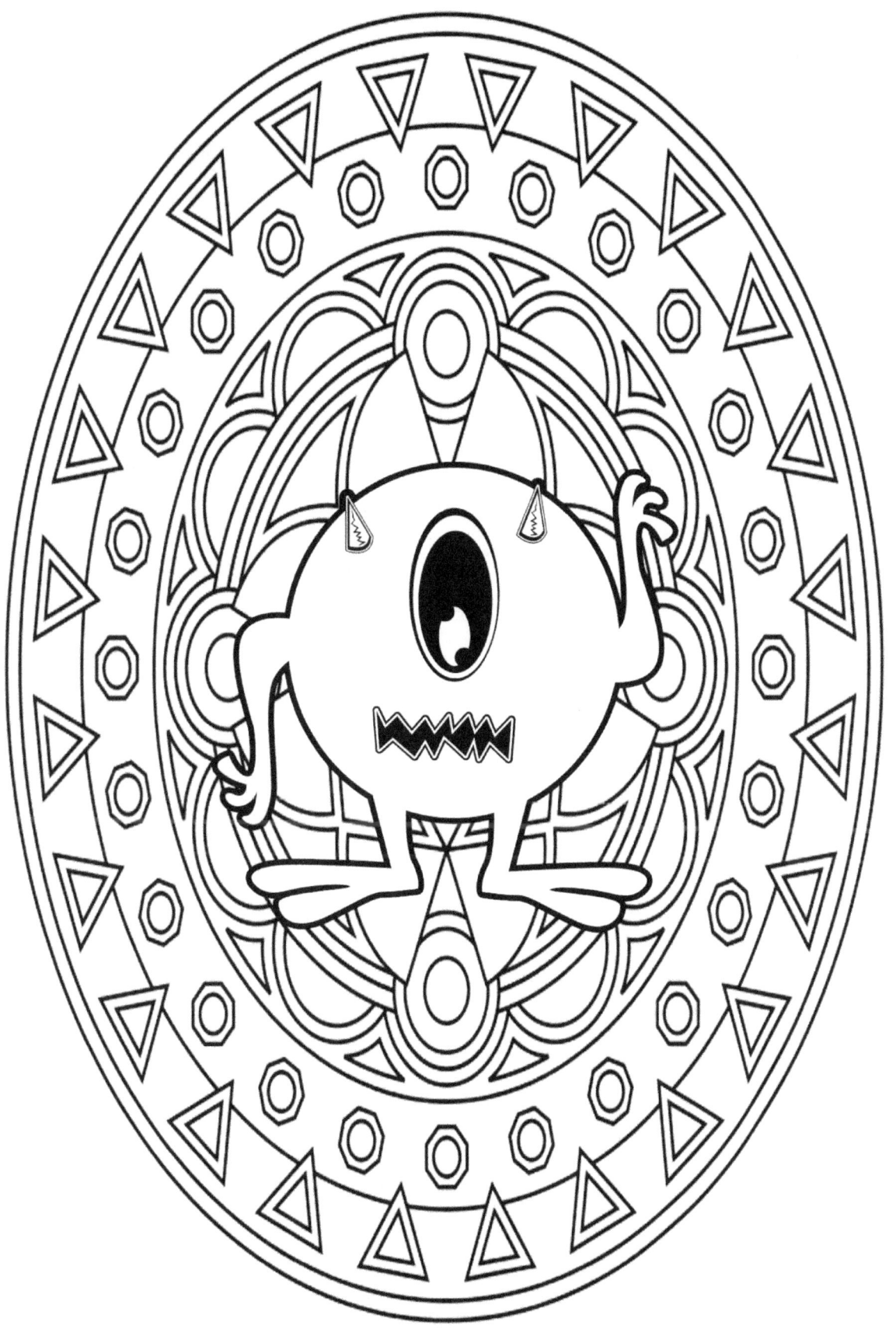

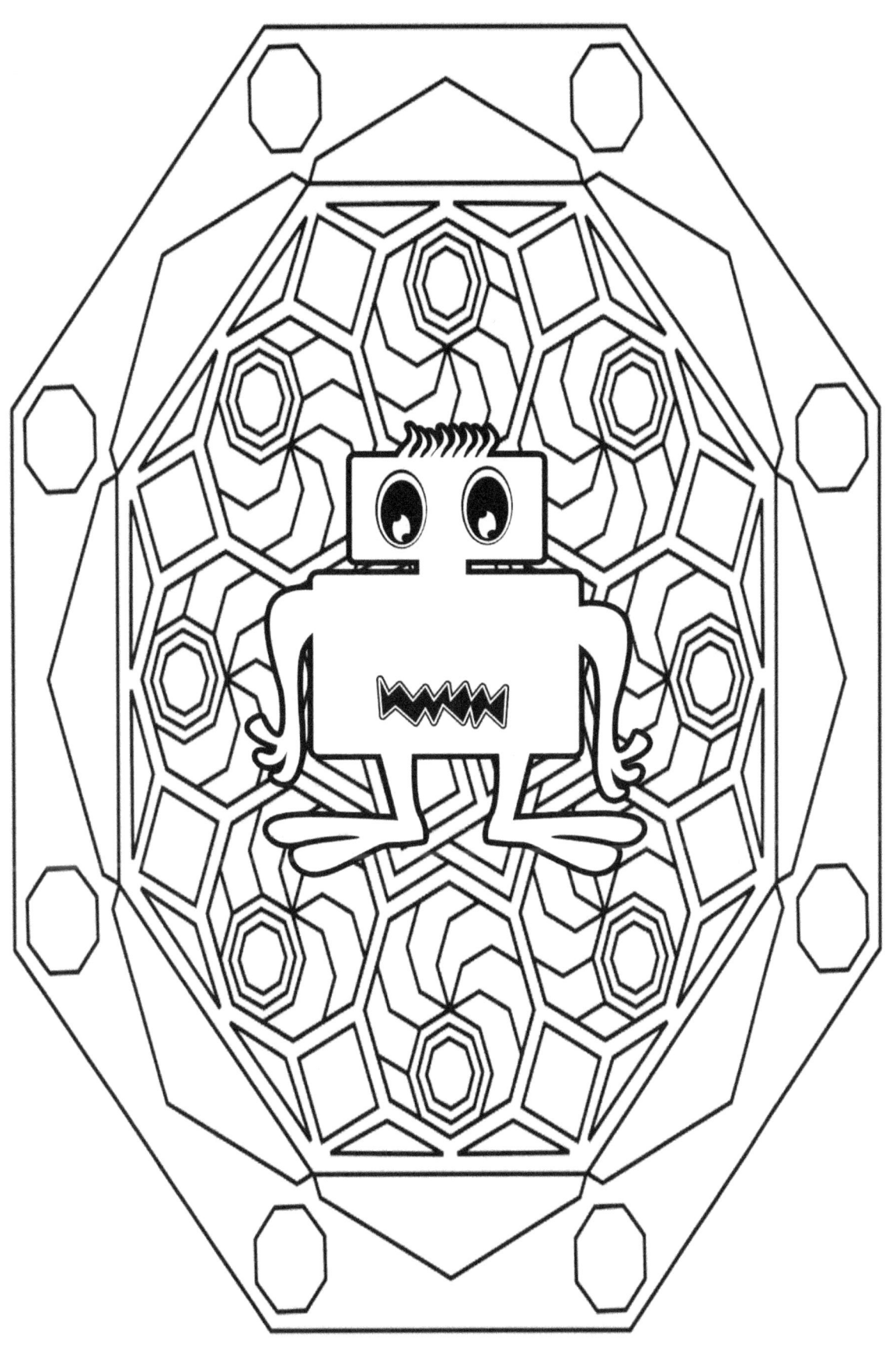

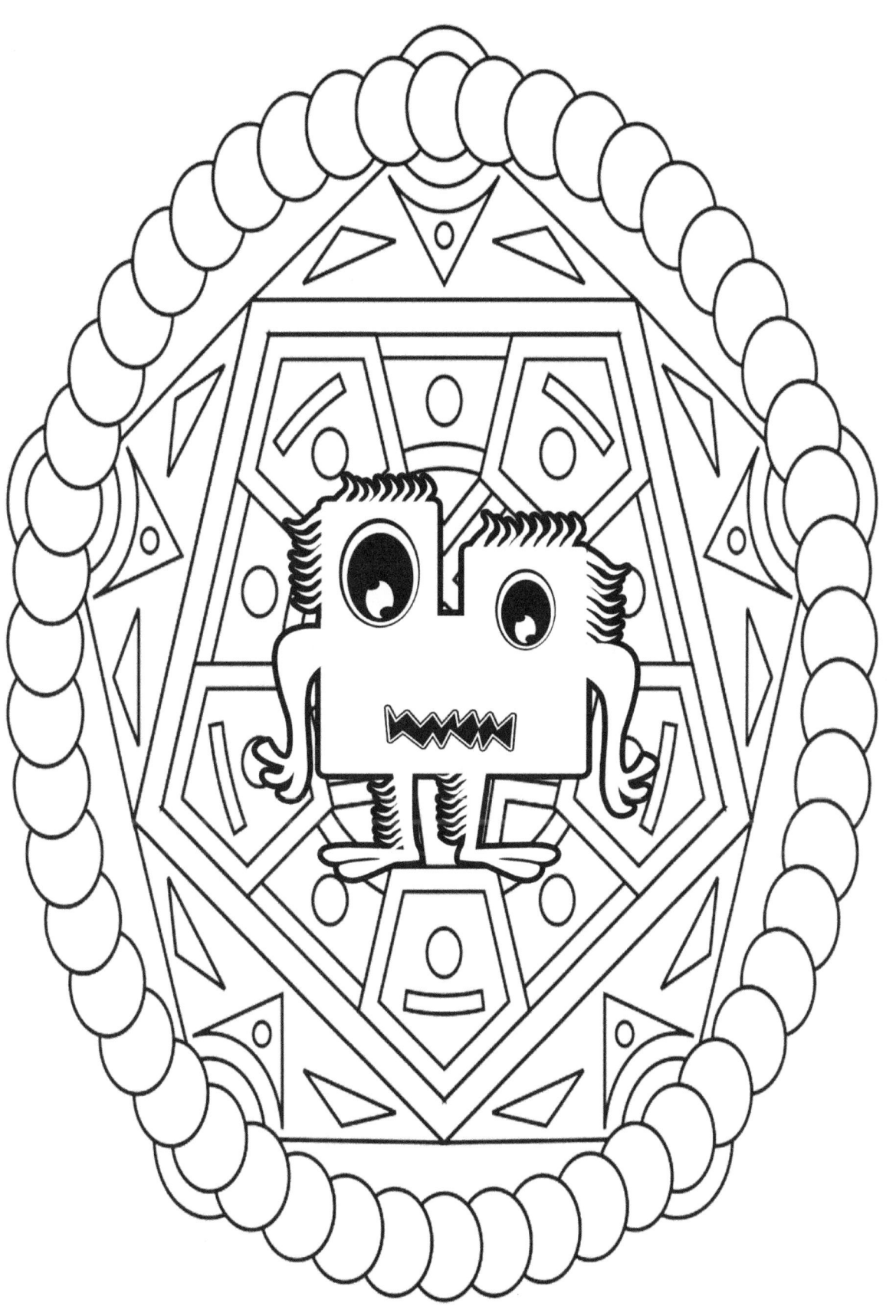

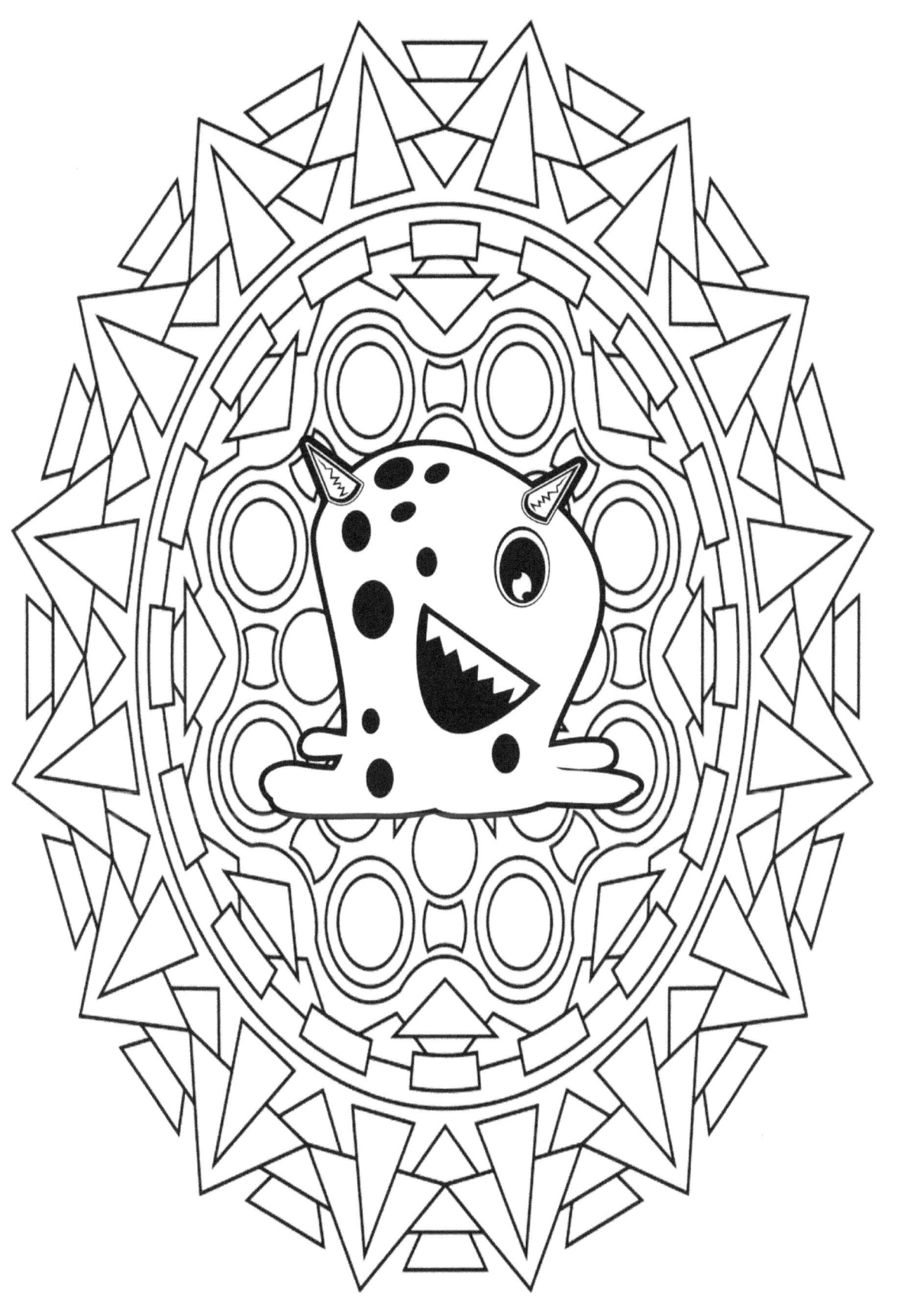

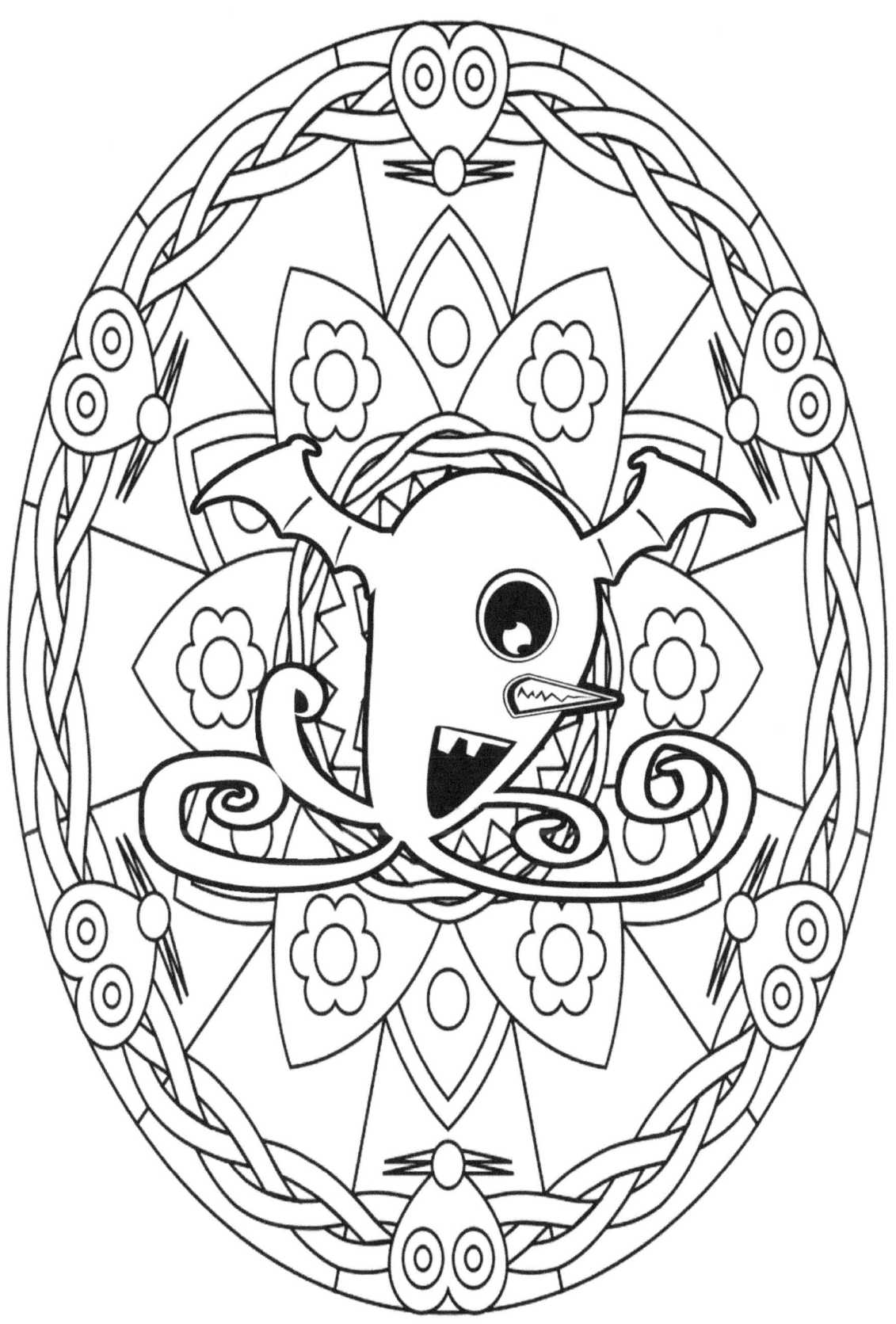

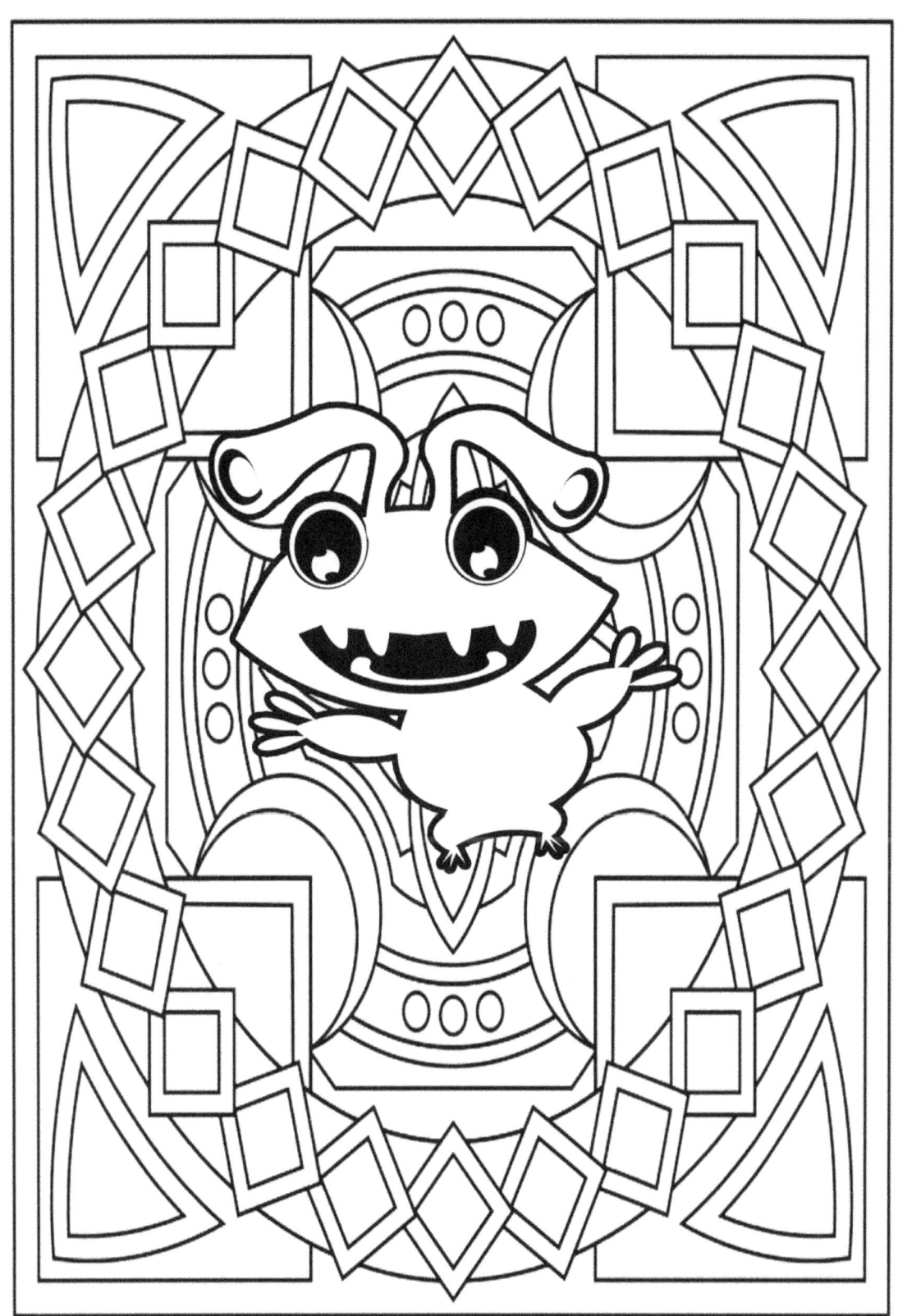

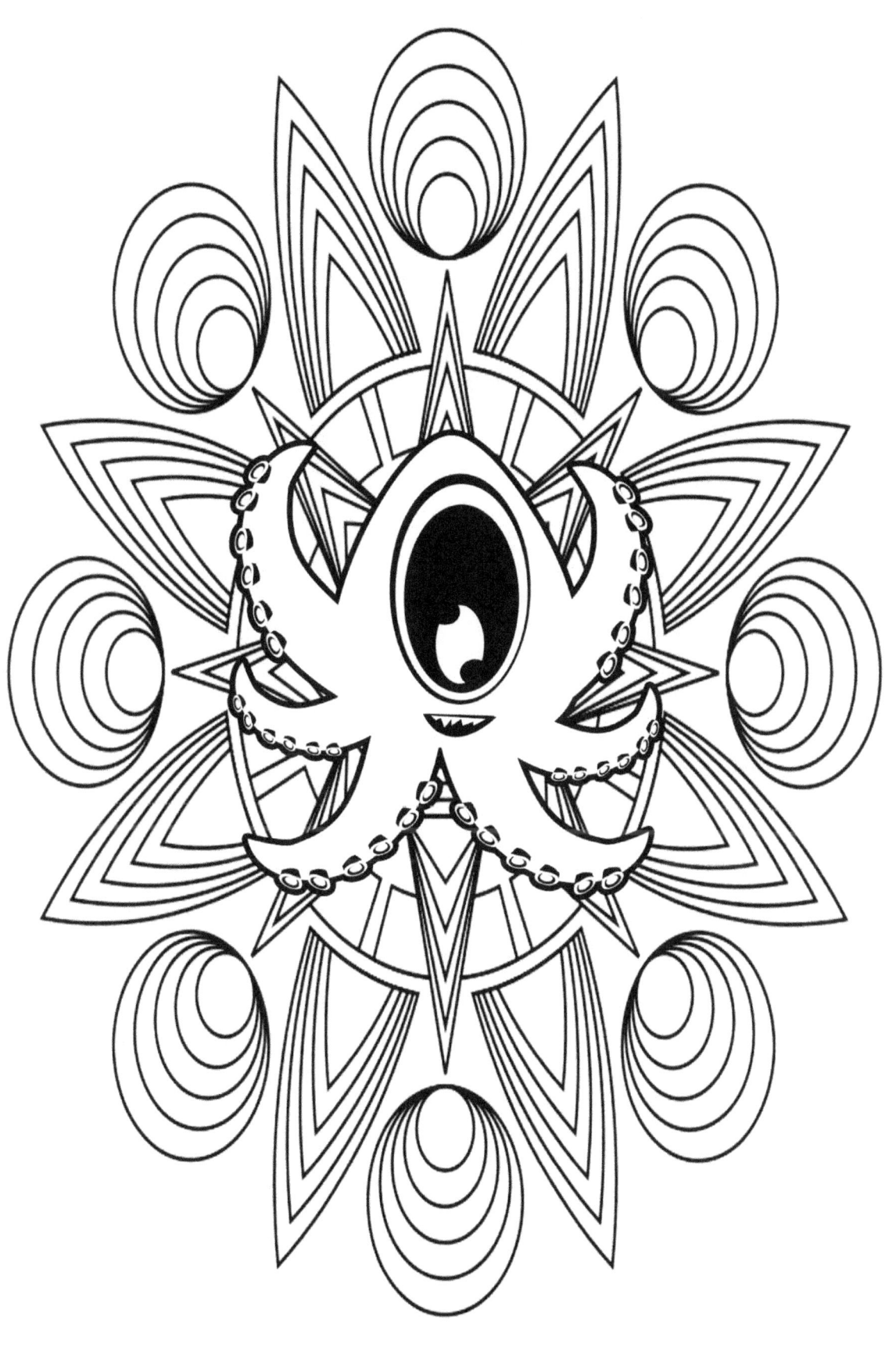

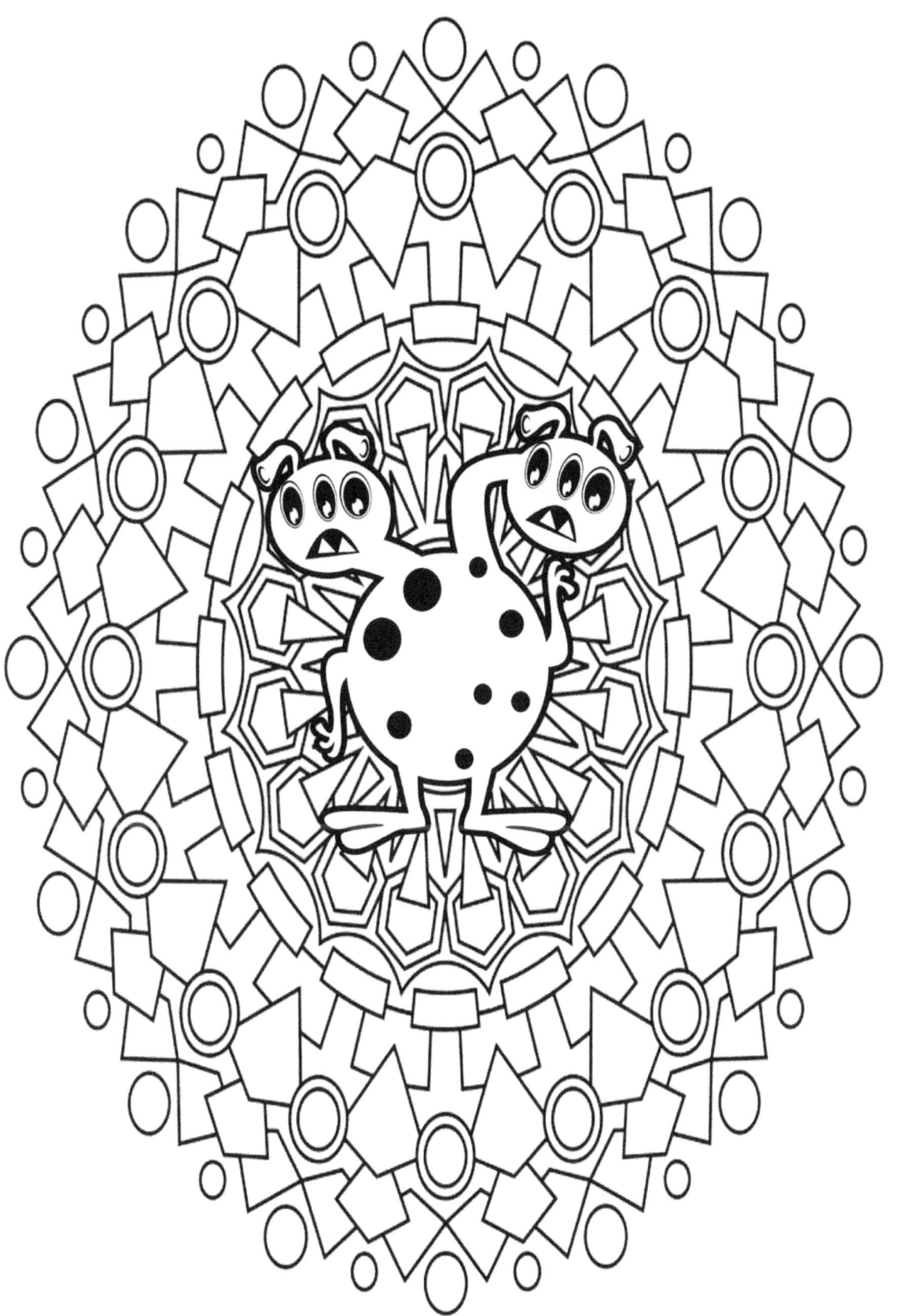

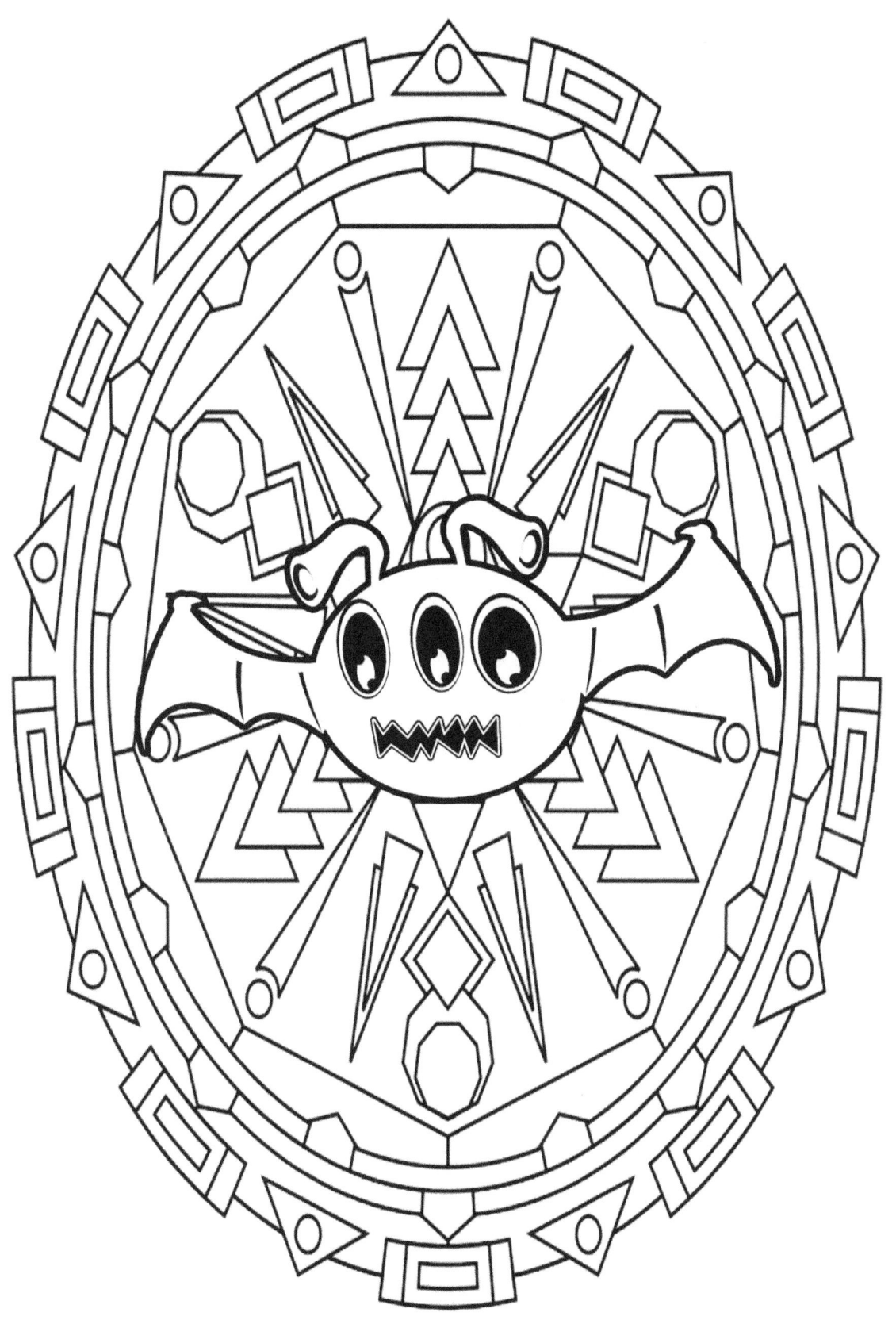

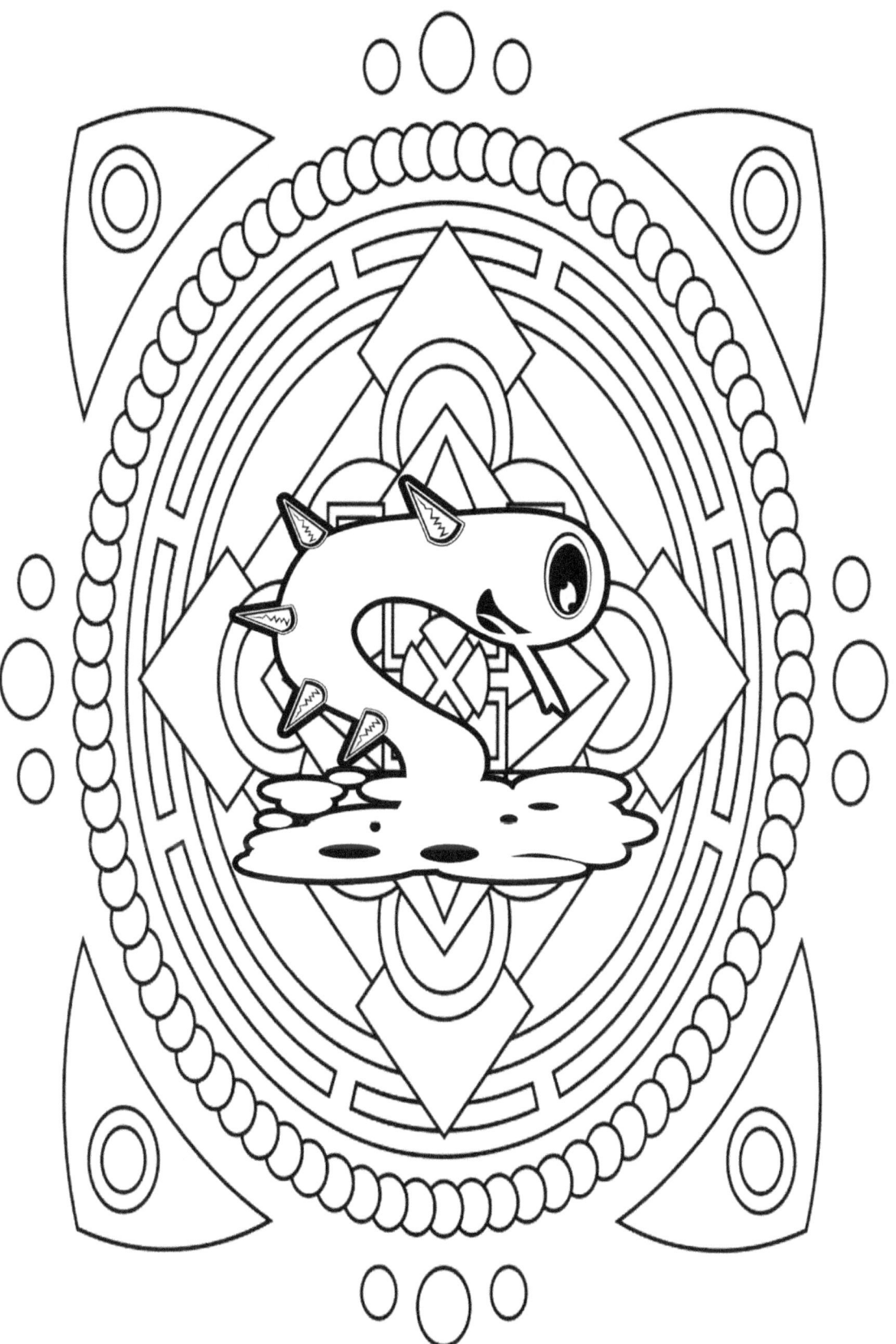

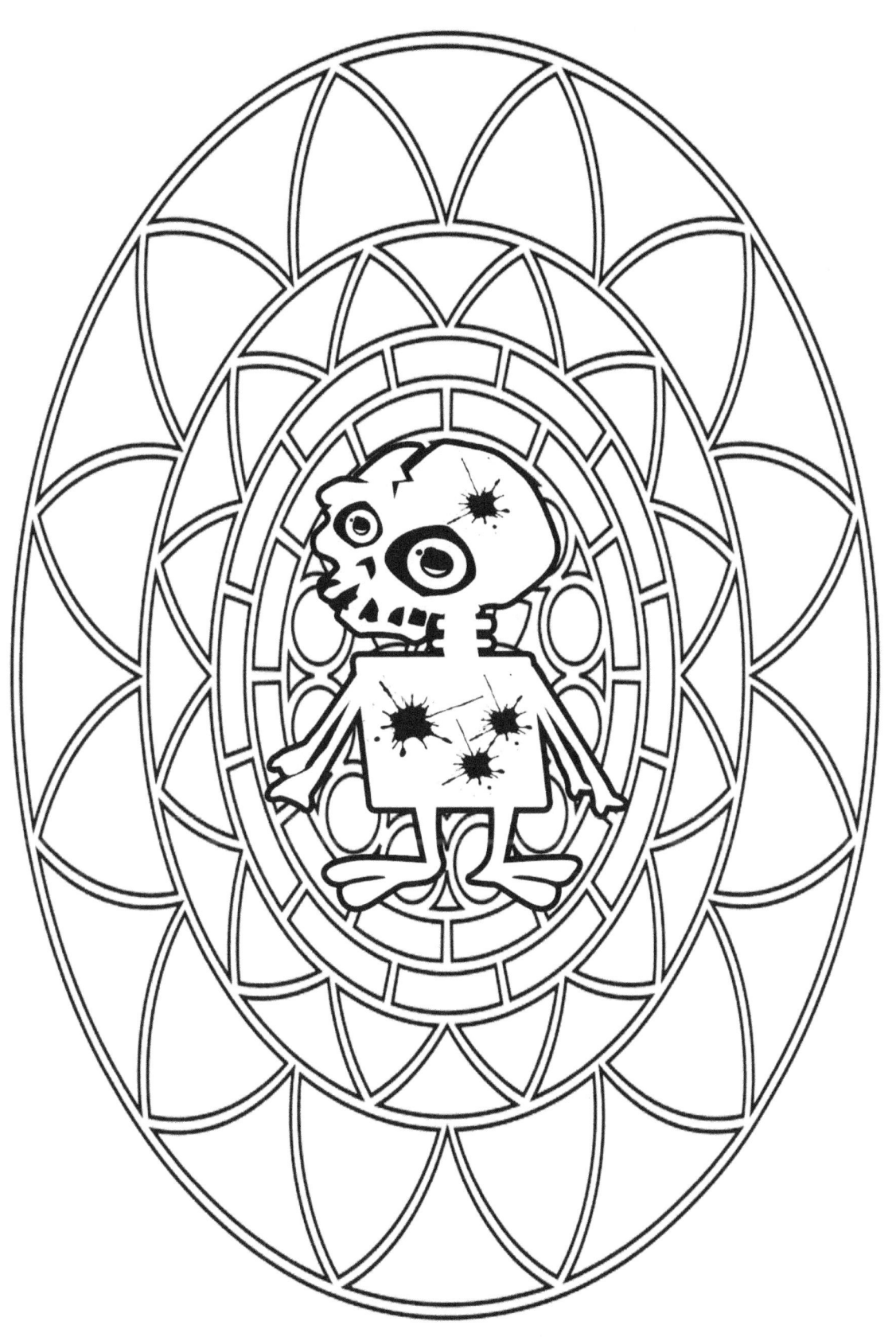

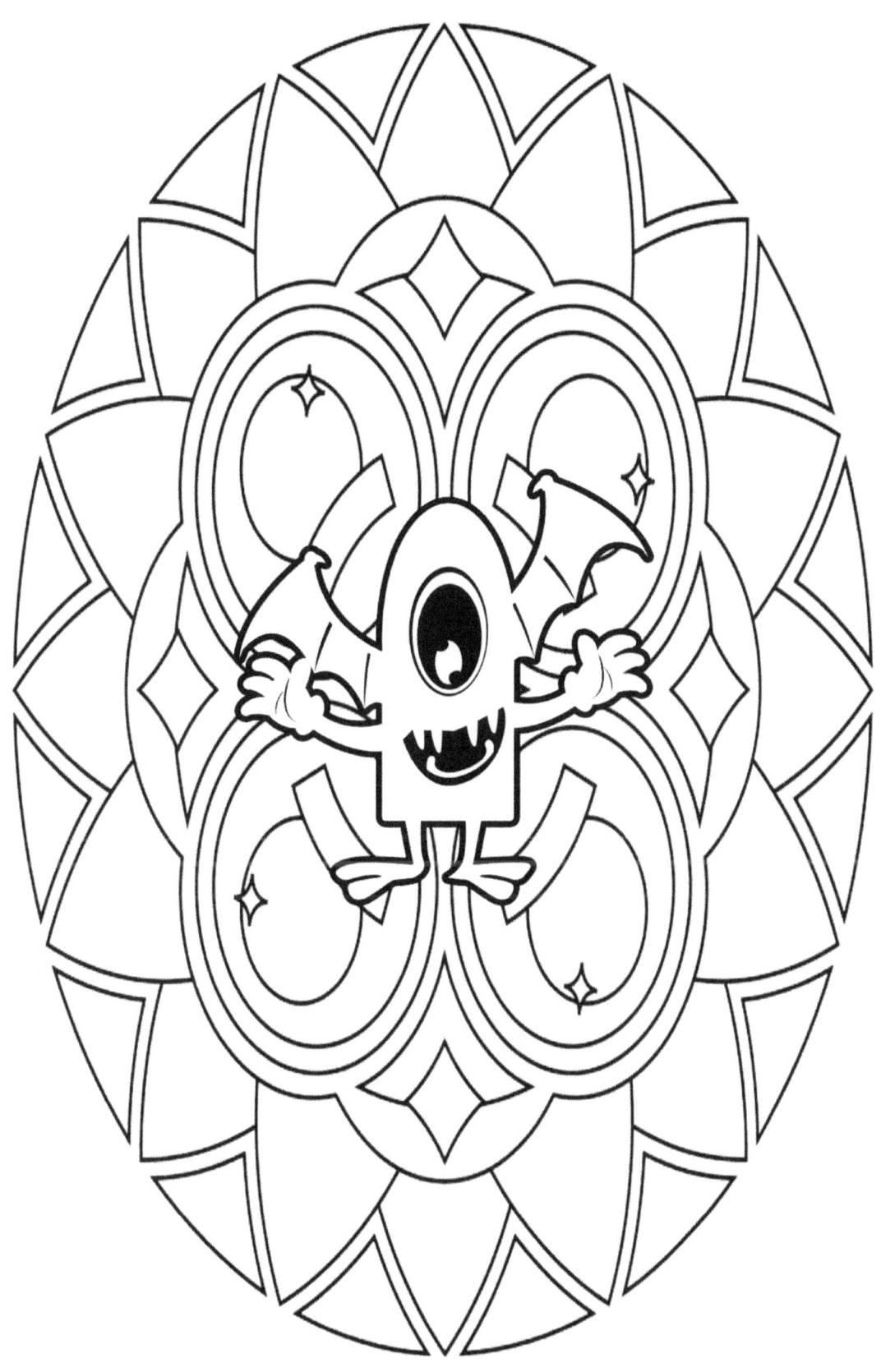

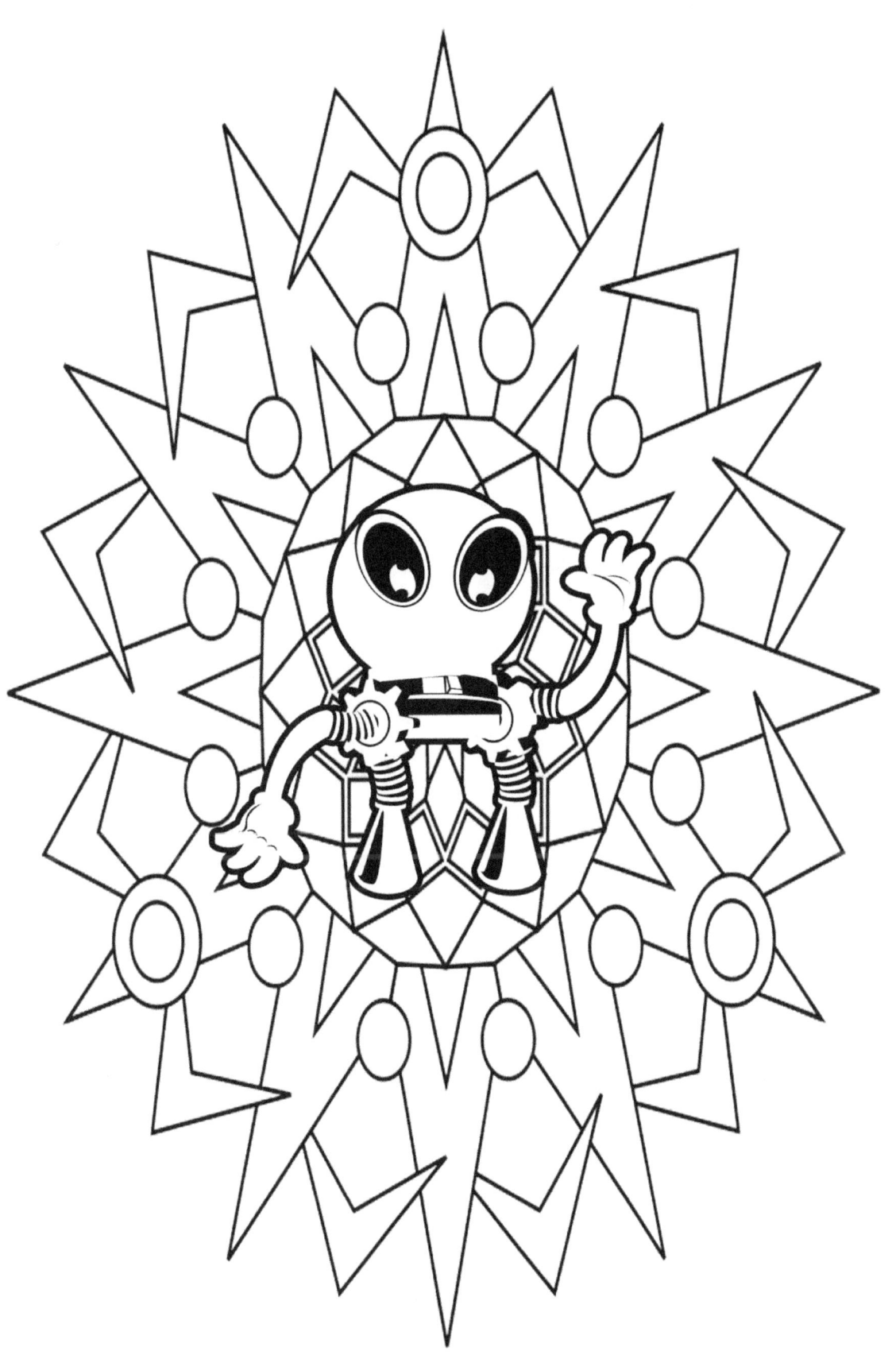

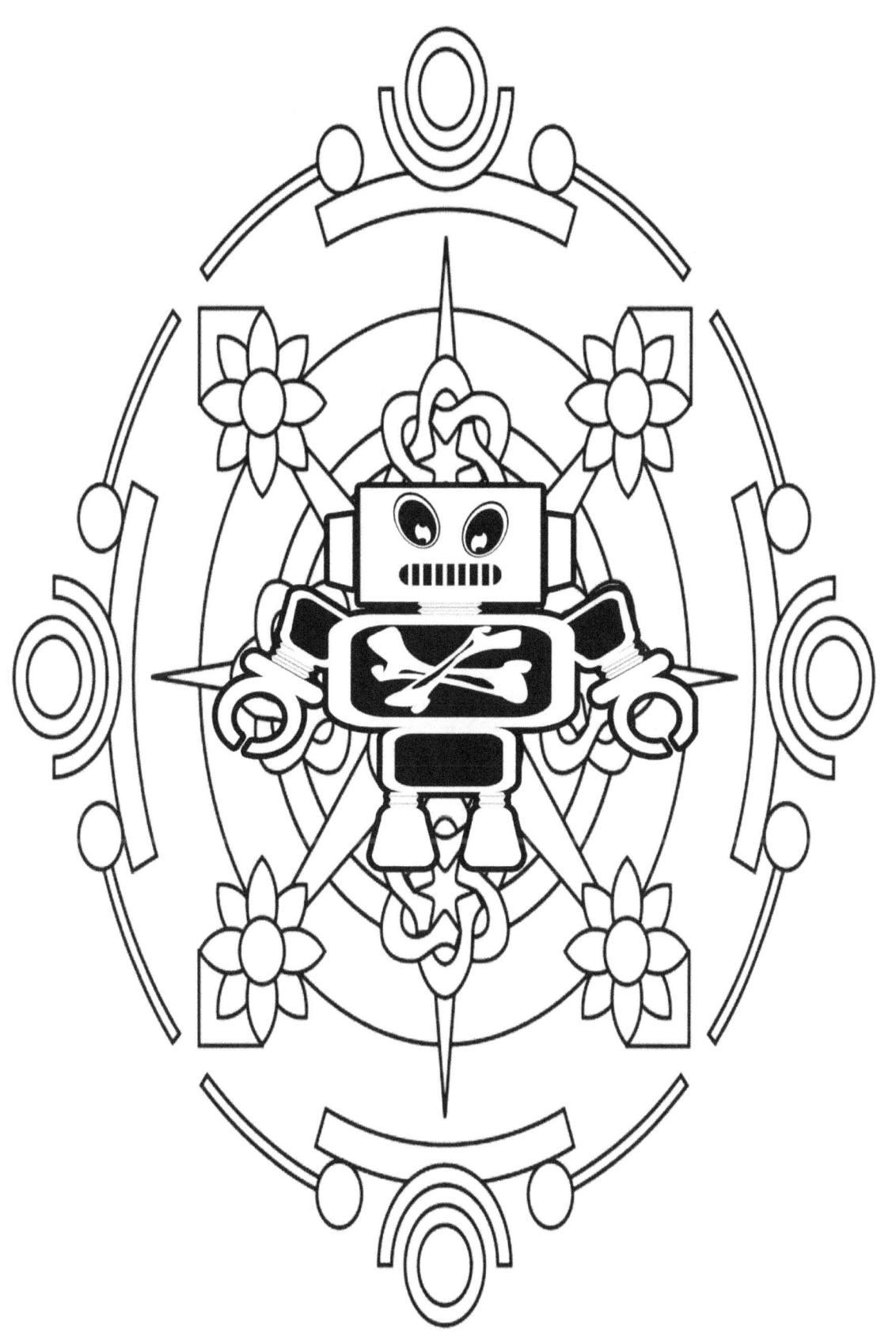

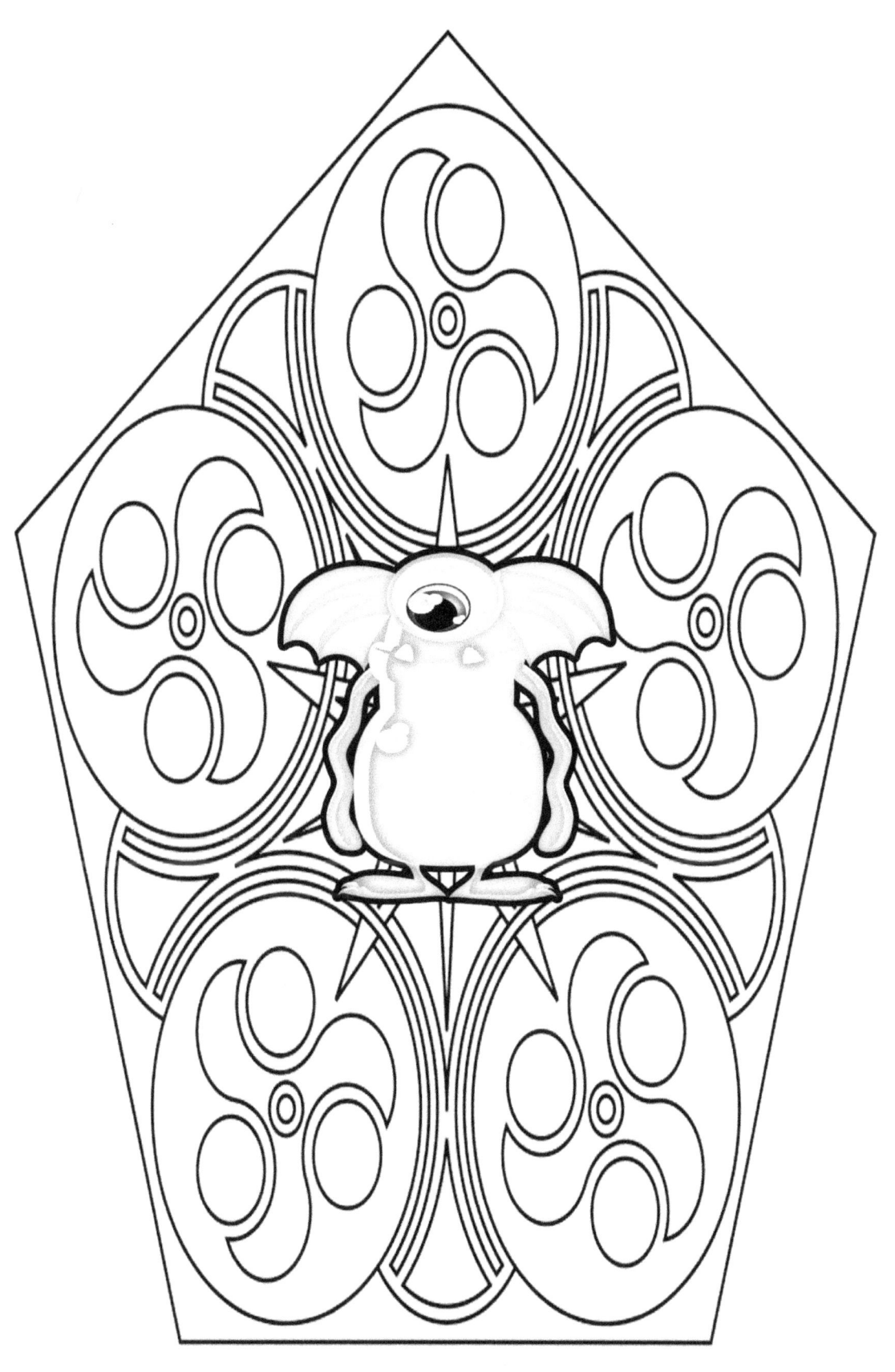

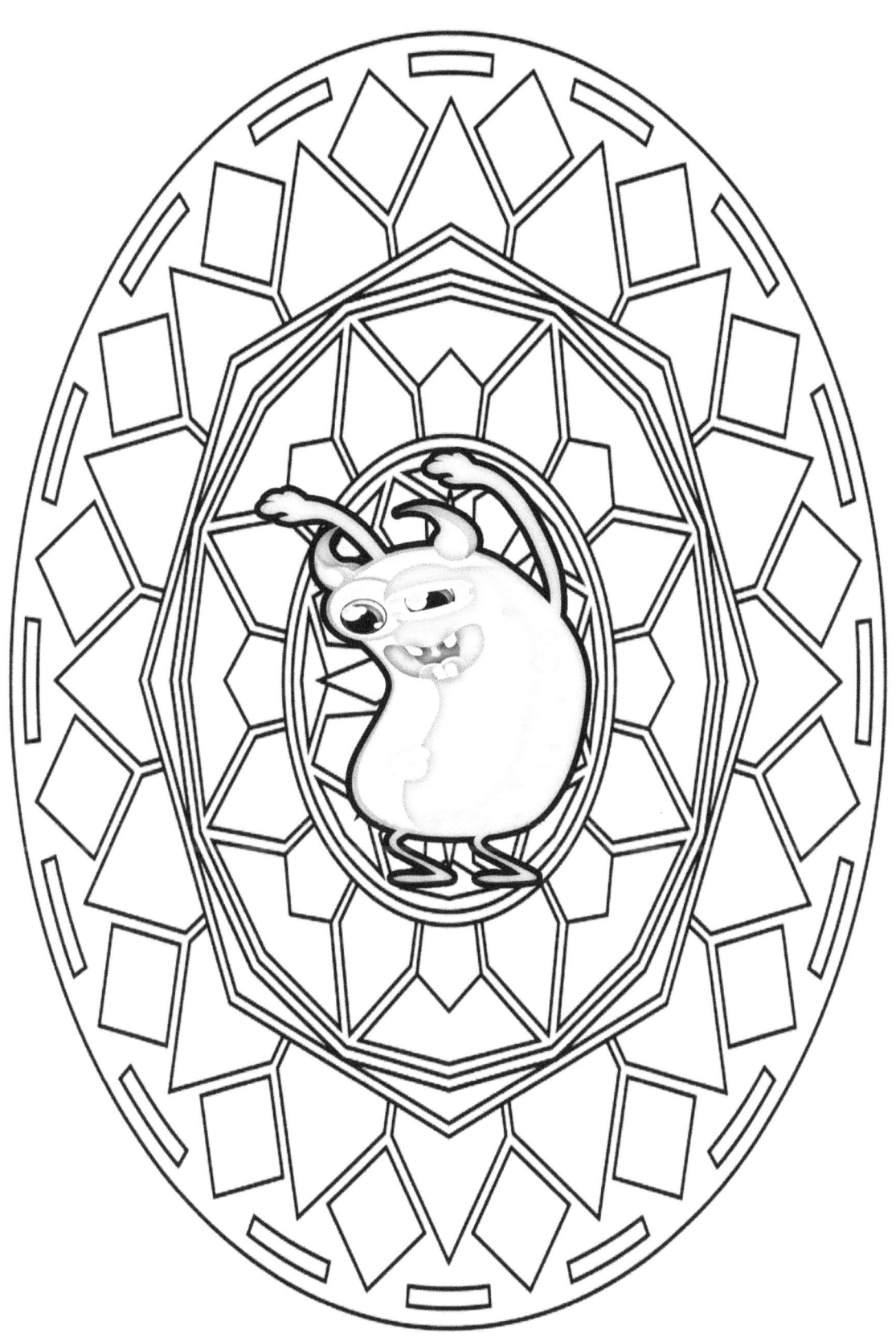

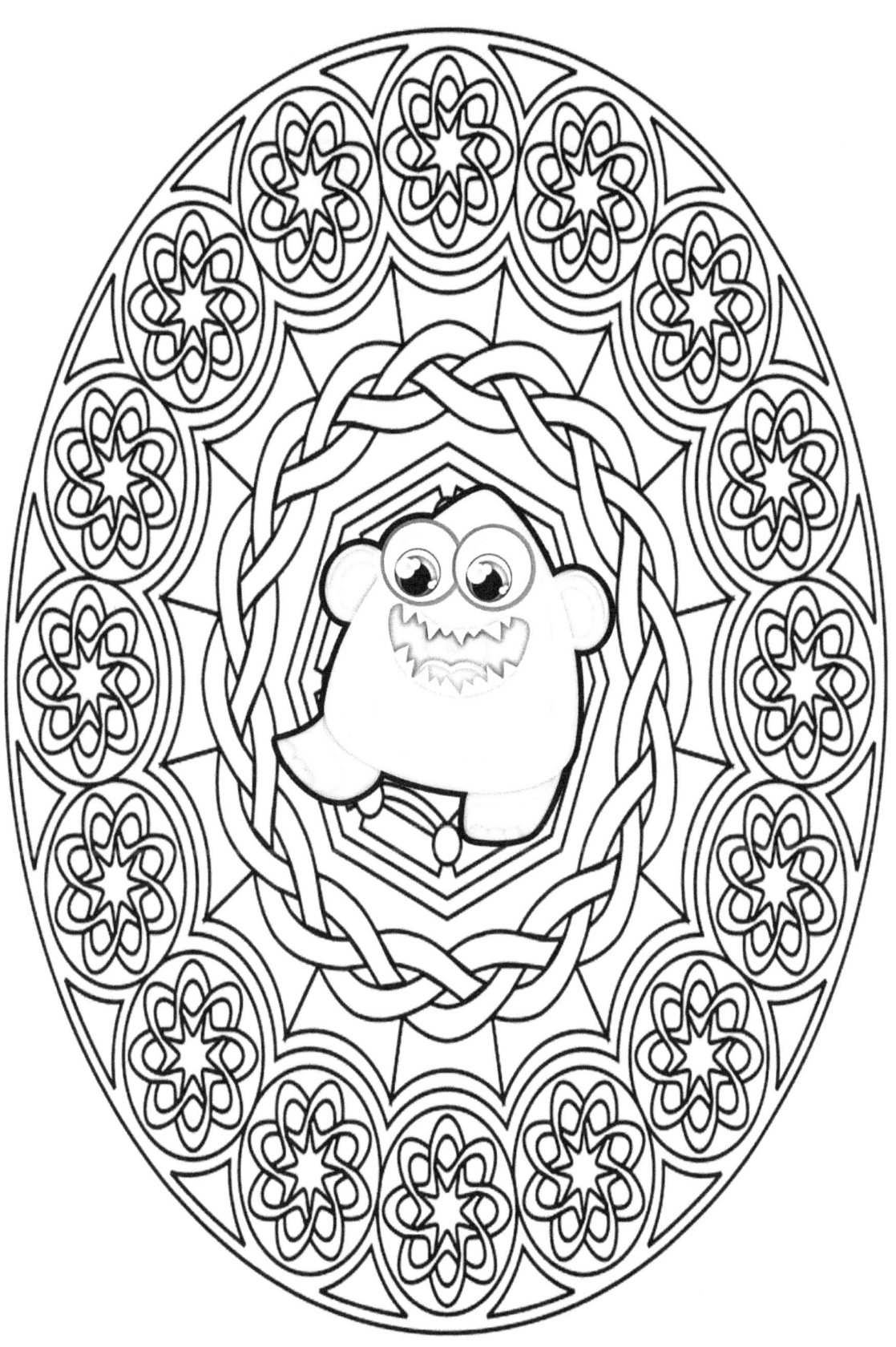

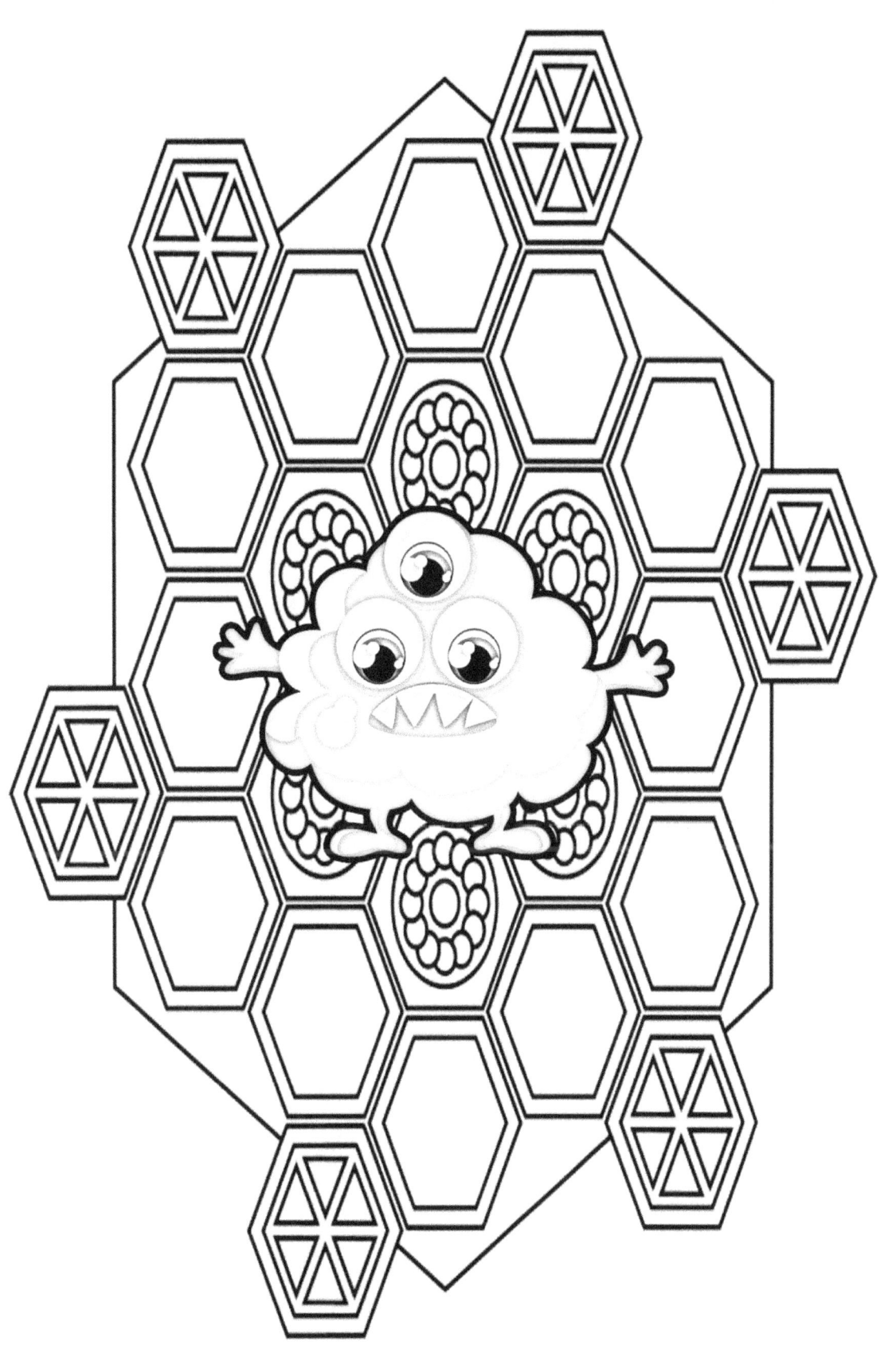

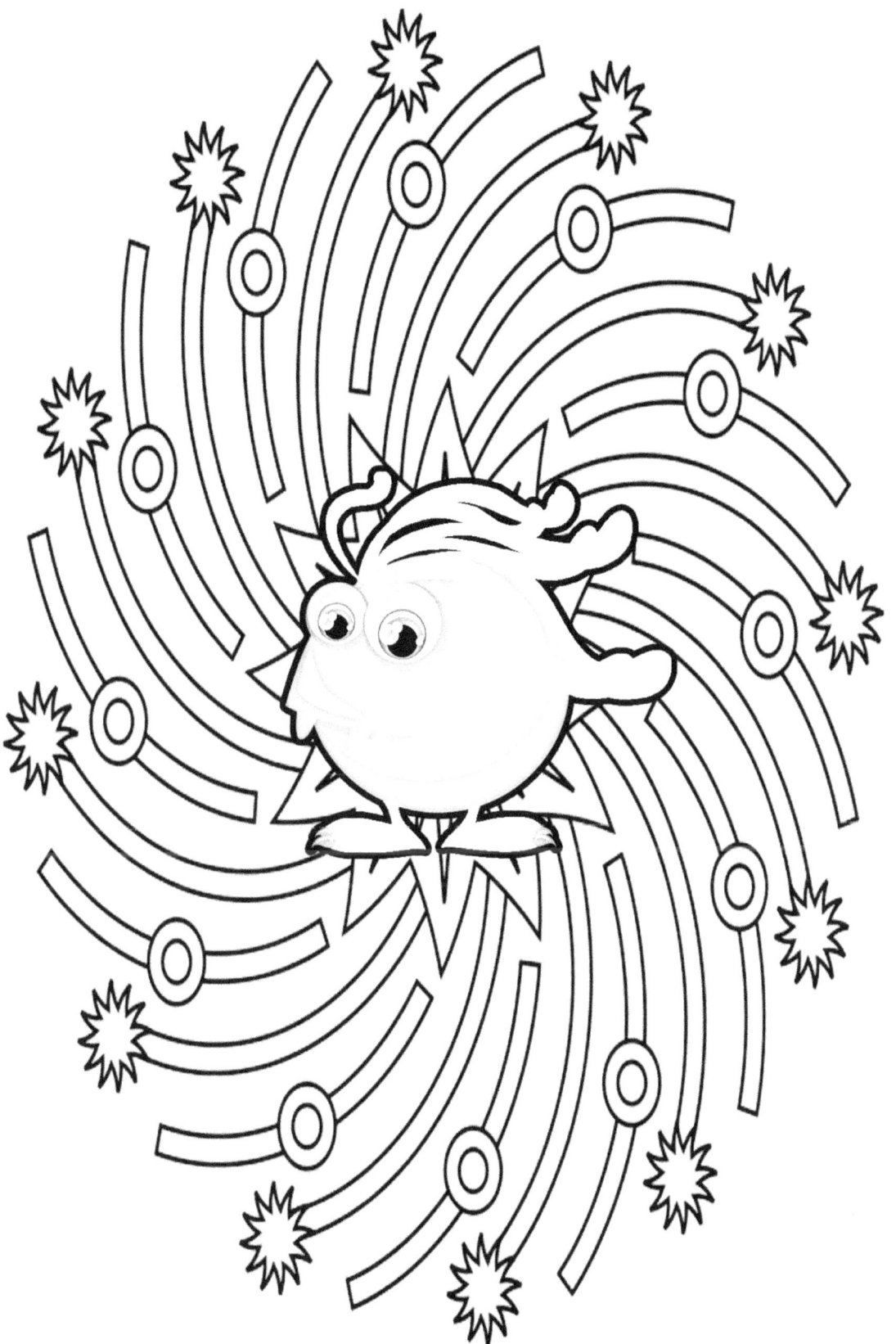

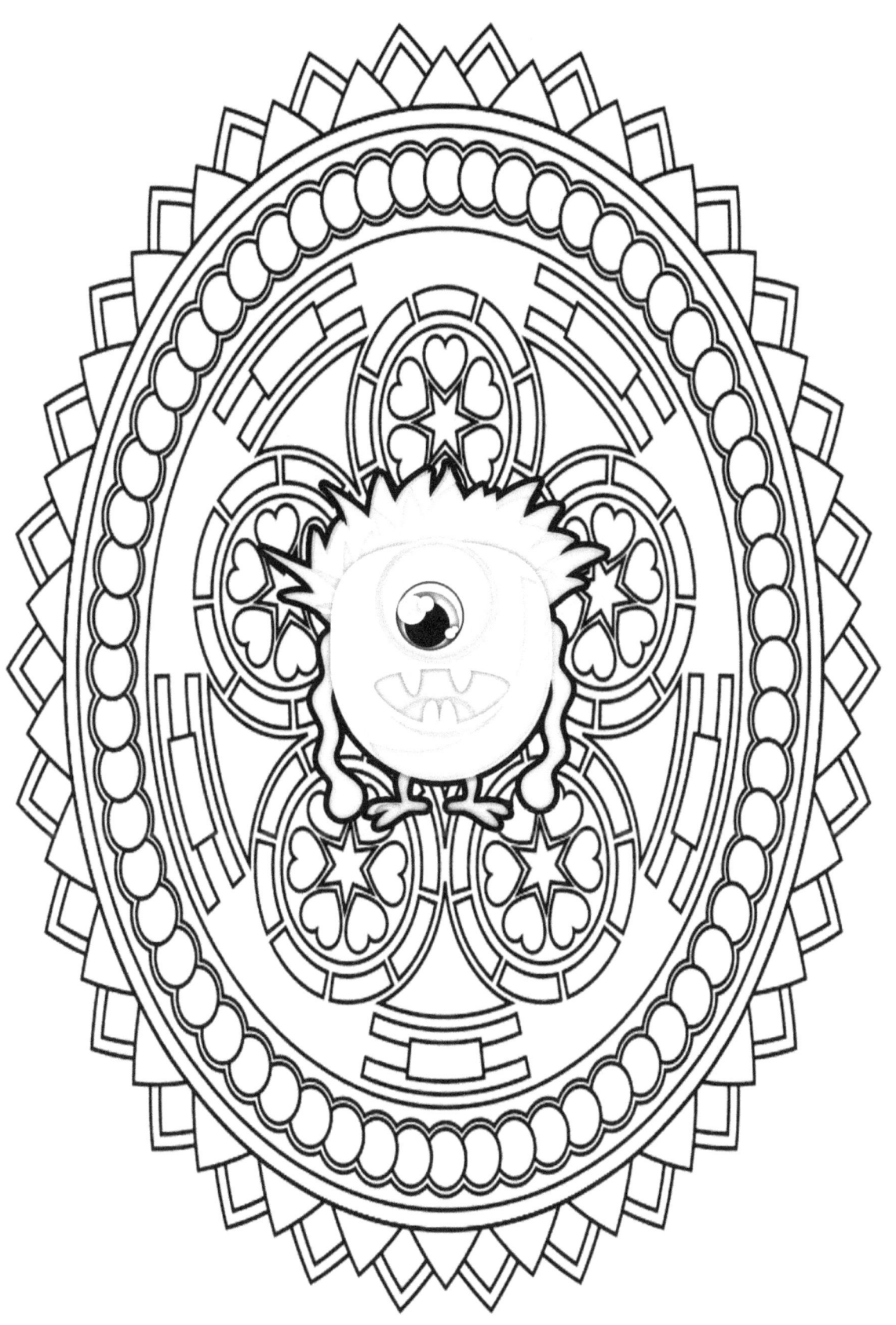

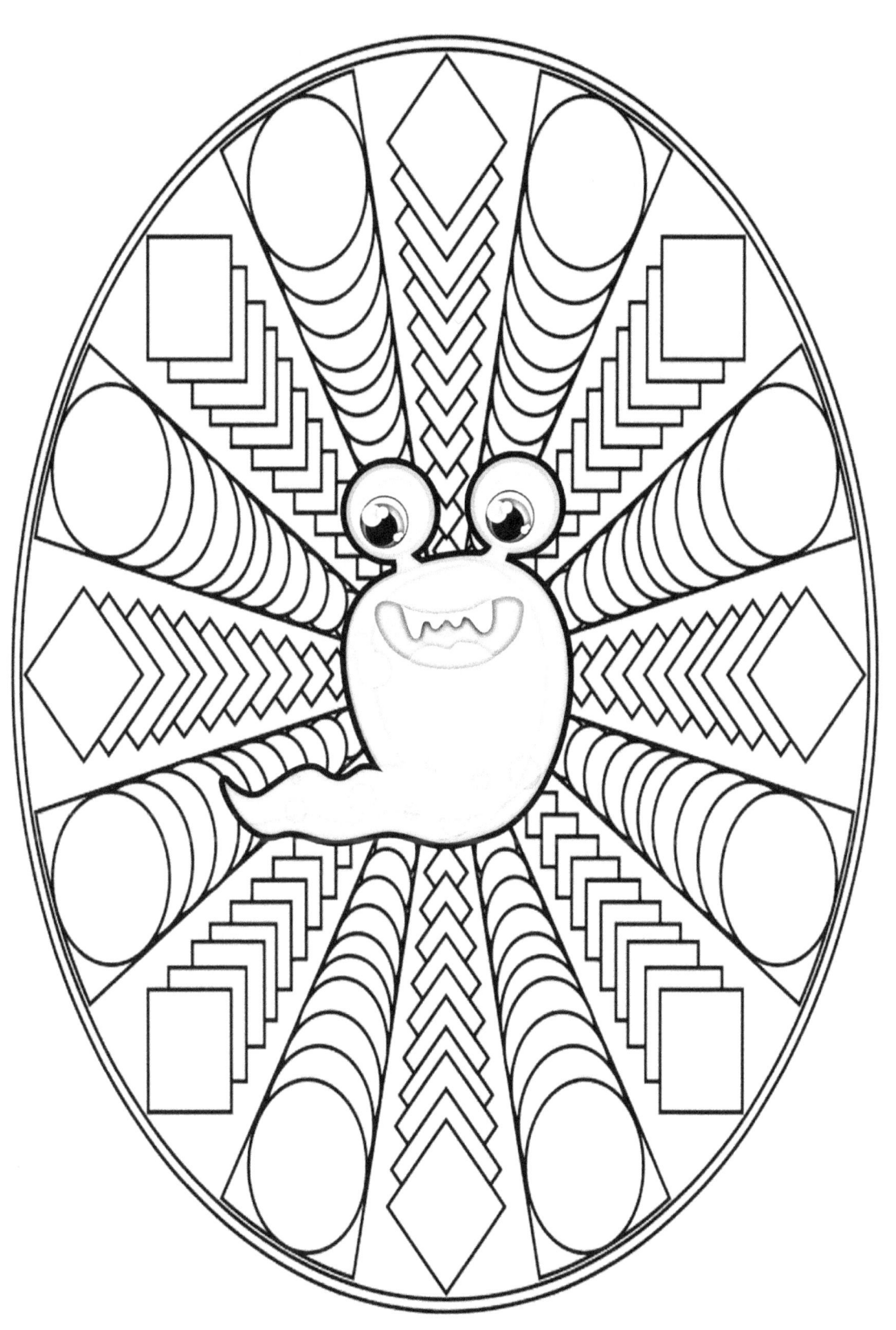

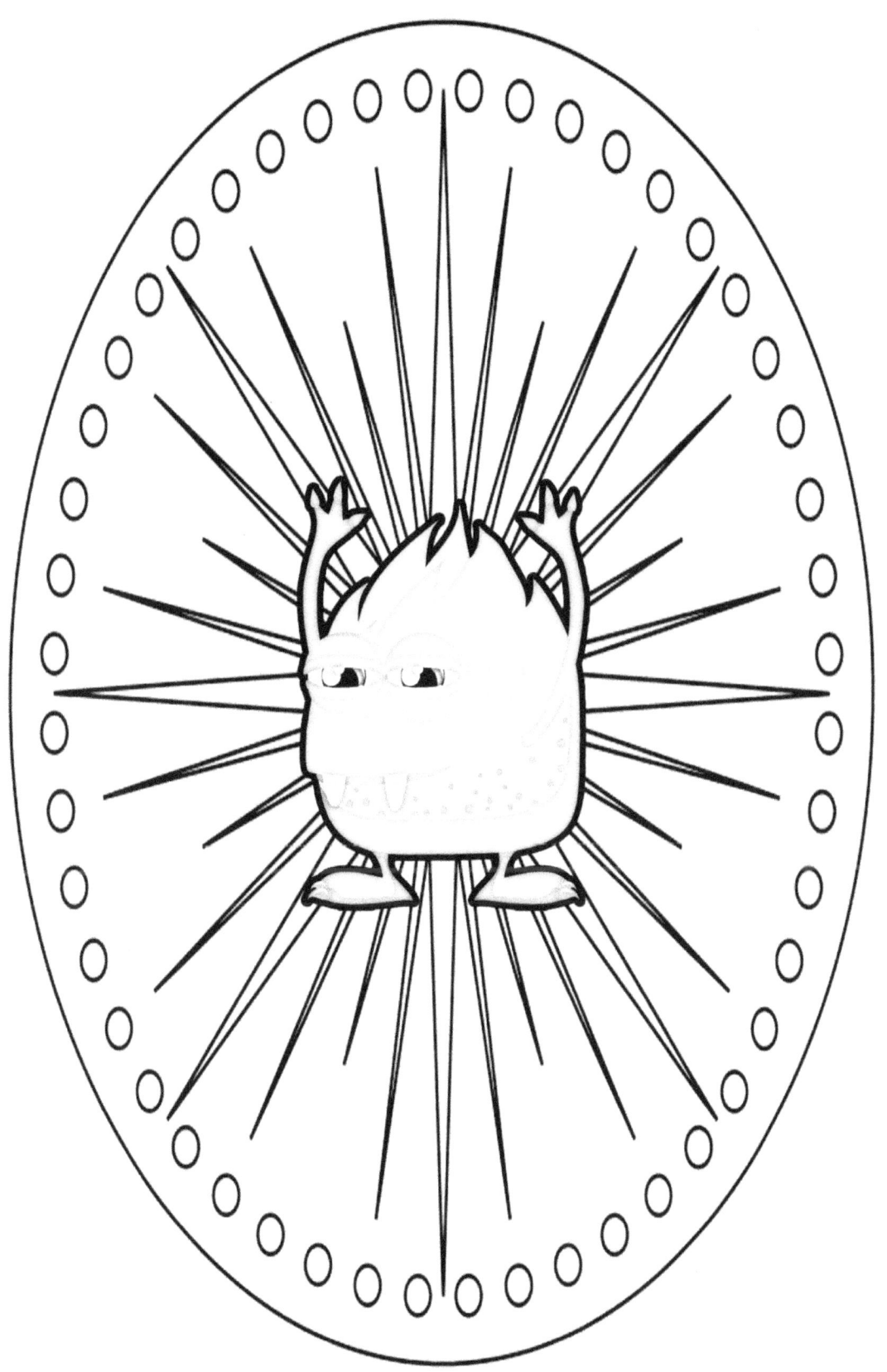

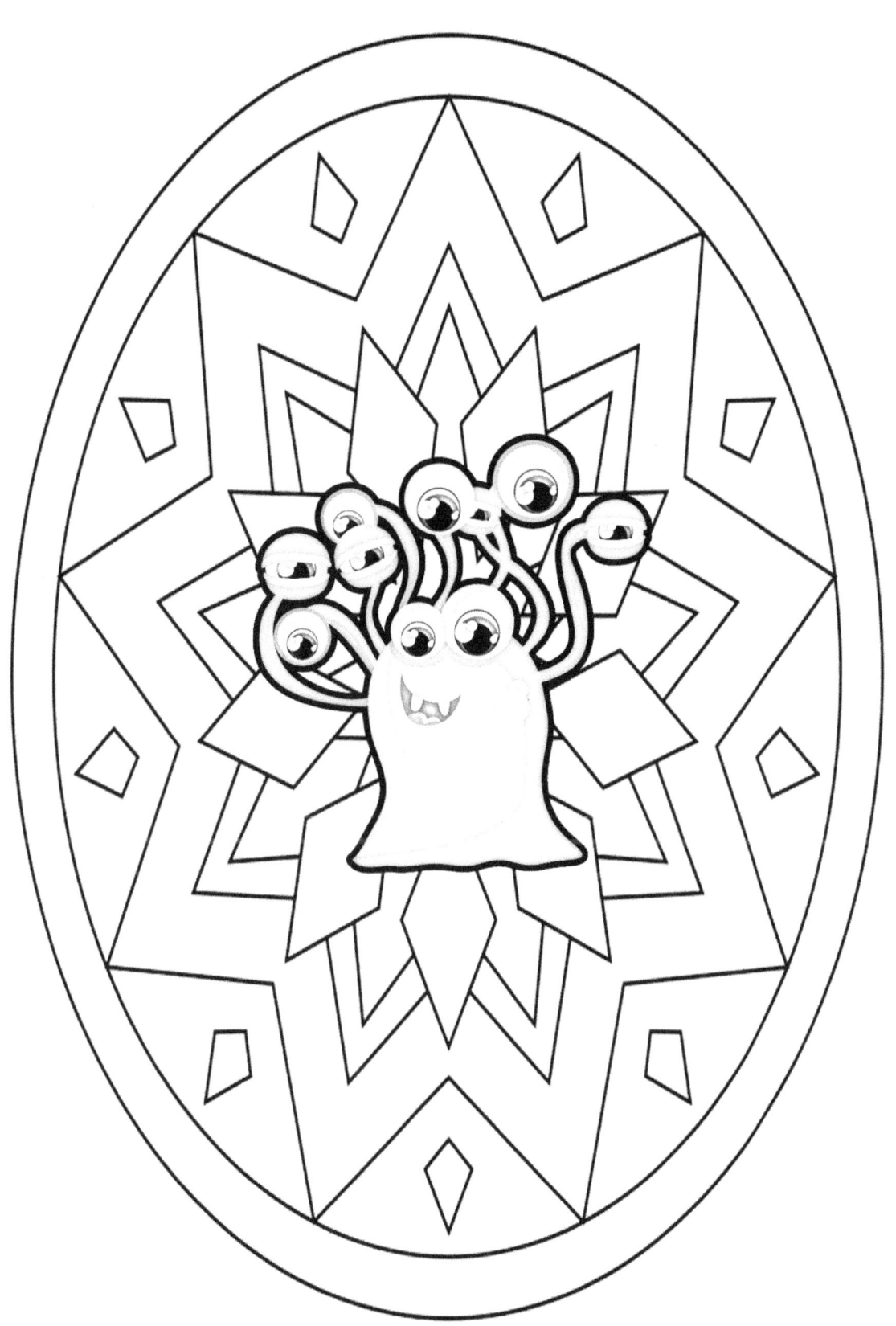

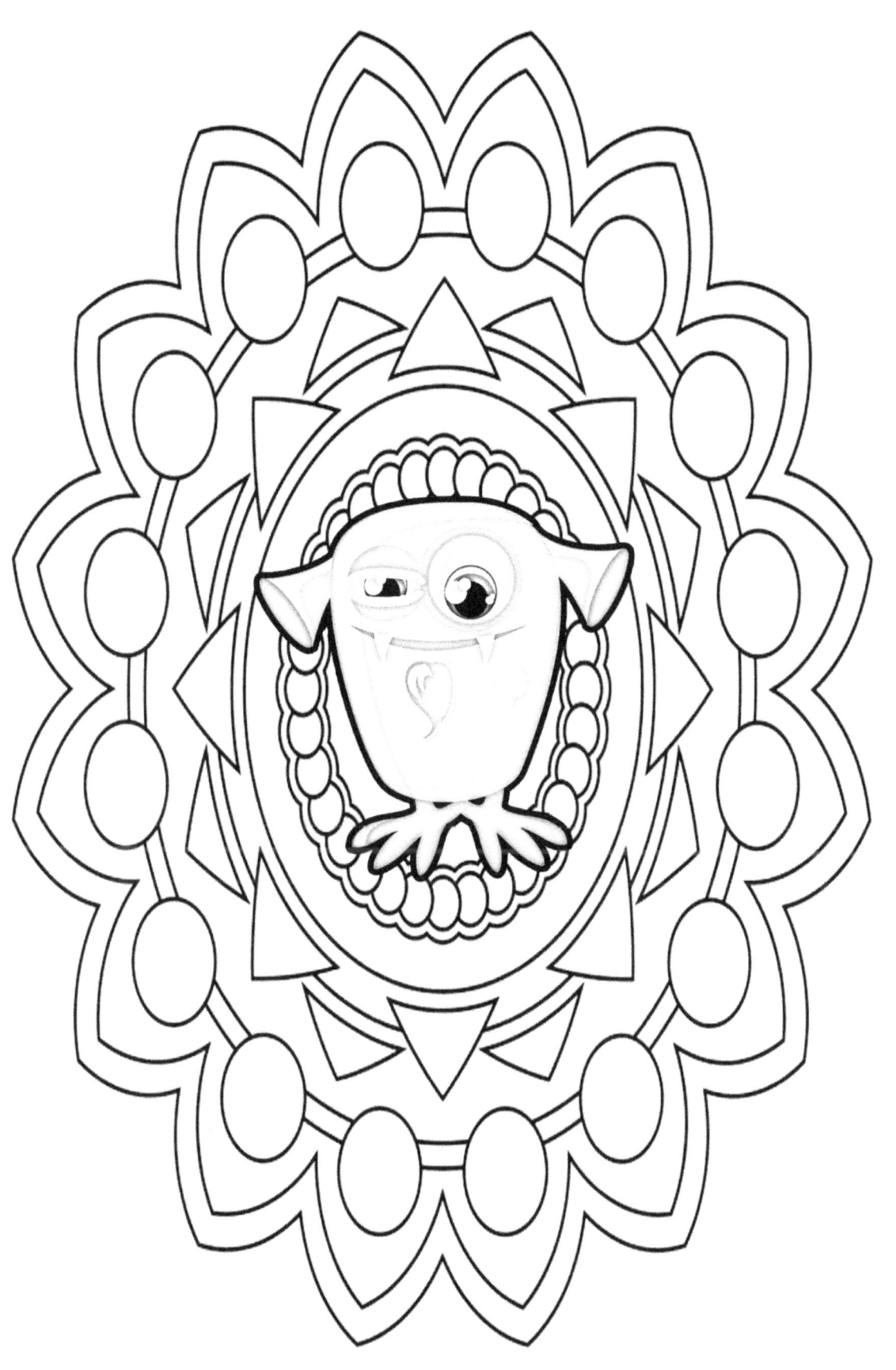

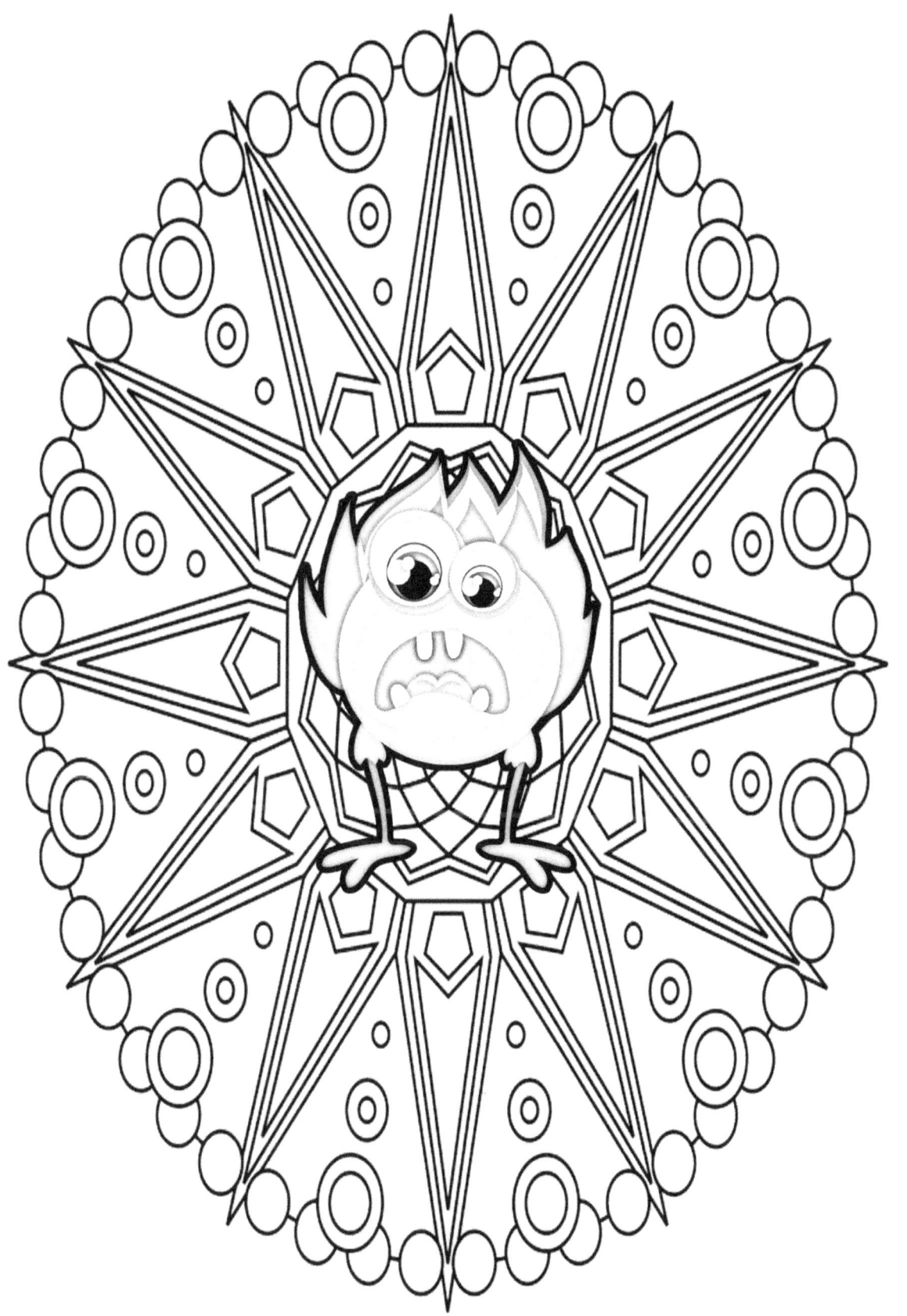

www.ingramcontent.com/pod-product-compliance
Lightning Source LLC
Chambersburg PA
CBHW080611180526
45168CB00007B/2863